Using EEG To Detect and Monitor Mental Fatigue

NASA Technical Reports Server (NTRS), et al., Leslie Montgomery

The BiblioGov Project is an effort to expand awareness of the public documents and records of the U.S. Government via print publications. In broadening the public understanding of government and its work, an enlightened democracy can grow and prosper. Ranging from historic Congressional Bills to the most recent Budget of the United States Government, the BiblioGov Project spans a wealth of government information. These works are now made available through an environmentally friendly, print-on-demand basis, using only what is necessary to meet the required demands of an interested public. We invite you to learn of the records of the U.S. Government, heightening the knowledge and debate that can lead from such publications.

Included are the following Collections:

Budget of The United States Government
Presidential Documents
United States Code
Education Reports from ERIC
GAO Reports
History of Bills
House Rules and Manual
Public and Private Laws

Code of Federal Regulations
Congressional Documents
Economic Indicators
Federal Register
Government Manuals
House Journal
Privacy act Issuances
Statutes at Large

Human.Systems 2001

Using EEG to Detect and Monitor Mental Fatigue

L. D. Montgomery, R.W. Montgomery
Lockheed-Martin

B. Luna, L. J. Trejo

NASA Ames Research Center, Moffett Field, CA 94035

Neuroengineering Laboratory

May, 2001

Presentation to be given at Human.Systems 2001: The Conference on Technologies for Human Factors and Psycho-Social Adaptation, NASA Johnson Space Center, June 20-22, 2001.

Title: **USING EEG TO DETECT AND MONITOR MENTAL FATIGUE**

Leslie Montgomery, Bernadette Luna, Richard Mongtomery, Leonard J. Trejo

Abstract (poster presentation)

This project aims to develop EEG-based methods for detecting and monitoring mental fatigue. Mental fatigue poses a serious risk, even when performance is not apparently degraded. When such fatigue is associated with sustained performance of a single type of cognitive task it may be related to the metabolic energy required for sustained activation of cortical areas specialized for that task. The objective of this study was to adapt EEG to monitor cortical energy over a long period of performance of a cognitive task. Multielectrode event related potentials (ERPs) were collected every 15 minutes in nine subjects who performed a mental arithmetic task (algebraic sum of four randomly generated negative or positive digits). A new problem was presented on a computer screen 0.5 seconds after each response; some subjects endured for as long as three hours. ERPs were transformed to a quantitative measure of scalp electrical field energy. The average energy level at electrode P3 (near the left angular gyrus), 100-300 msec latency, was compared over the series of ERPs. For most subjects, scalp energy density at P3 gradually fell over the period of task performance and dramatically increased just before the subject was unable to continue the task. This neural response can be simulated for individual subjects using a differential equation model in which it is assumed that the mental arithmetic task requires a commitment of metabolic energy that would otherwise be used for brain activities that are temporarily neglected. Their cumulative neglect eventually requires a reallocation of energy away from the mental arithmetic task.

Some Health Hazards in Long-Duration Missions

- Cephalad Fluid Shifts/Loss
  - Orthostatic intolerance upon reentry
  - Venous thrombosis
- Bone Demineralization
  - Fractures
  - Kidney stones
- Muscle Atrophy
  - Loss of strength
- Cardiovascular Deconditioning
  - Heart problems
  - Hypertension
- **Isolation/Confinement/Stress**
  - **Neurobehavioral dysfunction**
- Repetitive Motion Syndrome

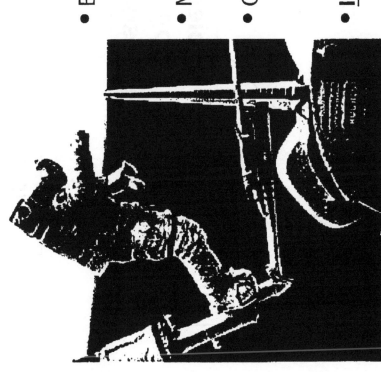

Cognitive Fatigue

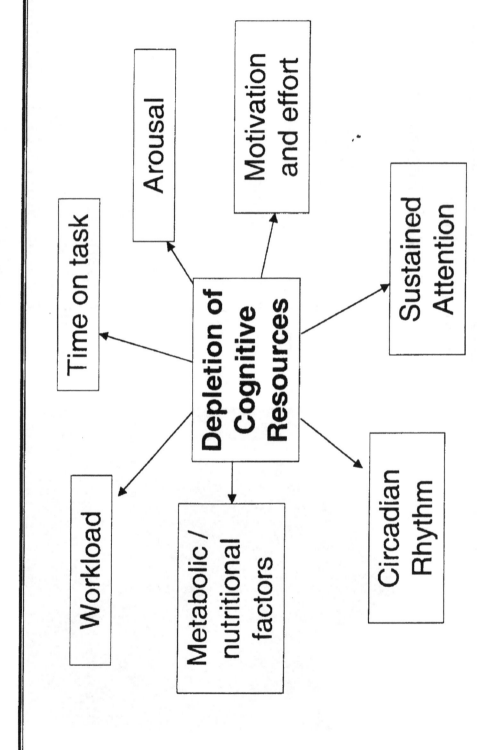

Previous Research

Multiple Sclerosis

- Evidence of EEG energy density correlations (Montgomery et al.)

- Krupp & Elkins (2000) - declines in single session

Lyme Disease

- Pollina et al. (1999) - cognitve deficits in speeded tasks, not seen in controls or depressed patients

Extended Wakefulness: ERP & Performance Studies

- Declines in early perceptual processes --'Humphrey, Kramer & Stanny (1994)

- Decreased effectiveness of error detection processes (Scheffers et al. 1999)

Mental Arithmetic Task

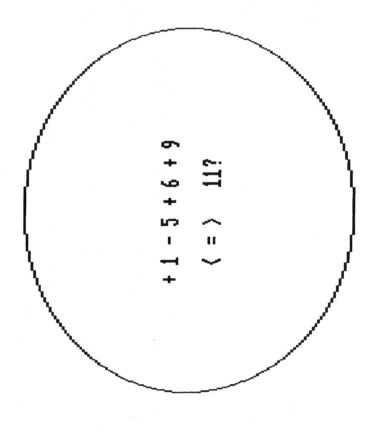

+ 1 - 5 + 6 + 9
< = > 11?

Electrode Locations

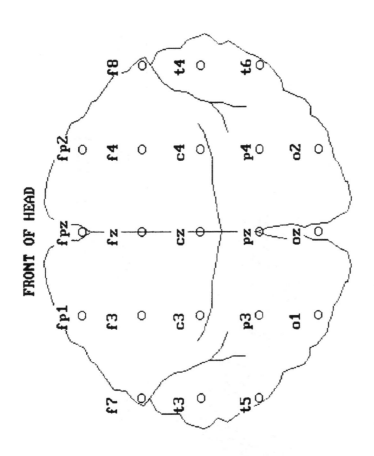

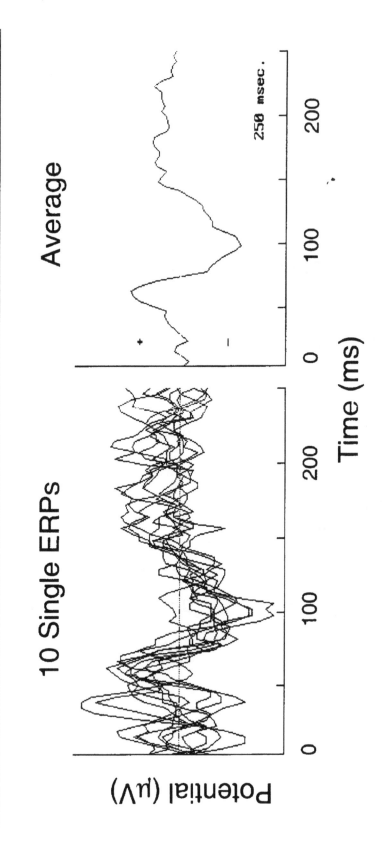

Sample EEG Surface Potential Distribution

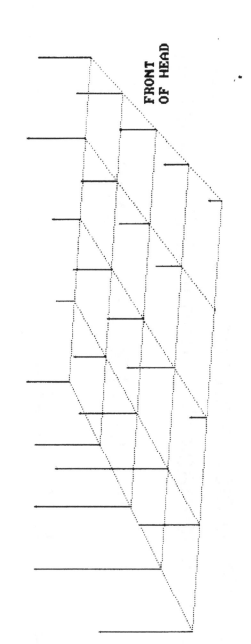

FRONT OF HEAD

Potential (μV)

2-D Projection of Electrode Location

Surface-Fitting Equation for Potentials

V = potential at electrode coordinates X, Y
X = side-to-side direction in 2-D projection
Y = front-to-back direction in 2-D projection

$$V = (a + bX + cY + dXY)^3$$

$$V = (b_1 + b_2X + b_3X^2 + \ldots\ldots + b_{15}X^2Y^3 + b_{16} X^3Y^3)$$

Derivation of EEG Energy Density Surface

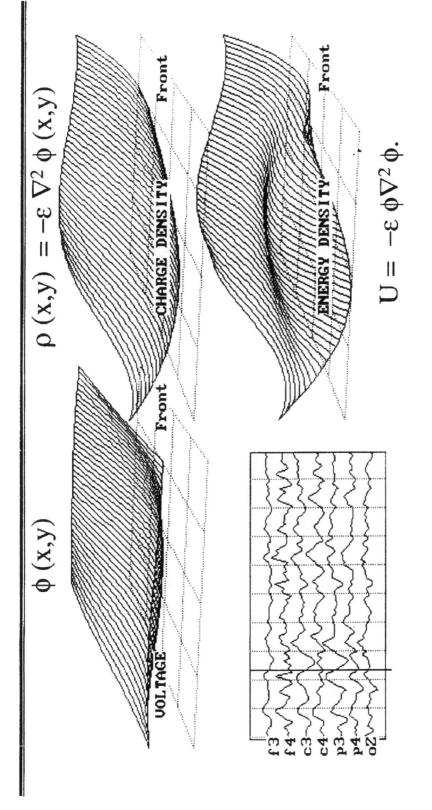

$\phi(x,y)$

$\rho(x,y) = -\epsilon \nabla^2 \phi(x,y)$

VOLTAGE

Front

CHARGE DENSITY

Front

ENERGY DENSITY

Front

$U = -\epsilon \phi \nabla^2 \phi.$

f3
f4
c3
c4
p3
p4
oz

Average Maxima of Measured Energy Density

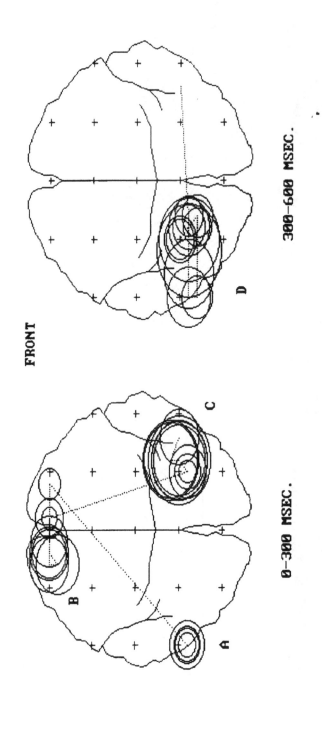

Task Error Index vs. Energy Density

Index = RT × (1 + wrong / n)

Electrode	Period (ms)	r^2	Slope T
T5	47-86	0.913	-5.624
T5	55-94	0.948	-7.402
FPZ	86-126	0.877	-4.624
FPZ	94-133	0.897	-5.122
F3	102-141	0.878	-4.639
FPZ	110-149	0.856	-4.609
FPZ	118-157	0.876	-4.223
P4	141-180	0.851	4.134
P4	149-188	0.878	4.657
P4	157-196	0.882	4.740
P4	165-204	0.869	4.458
T5	172-211	0.914	-5.637

Group Performance vs. Energy Density

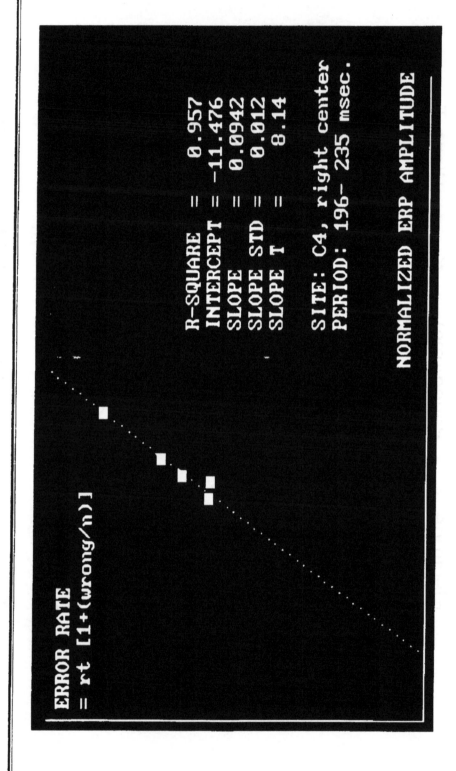

Performance & Energy Density Over Time
Normal Subject

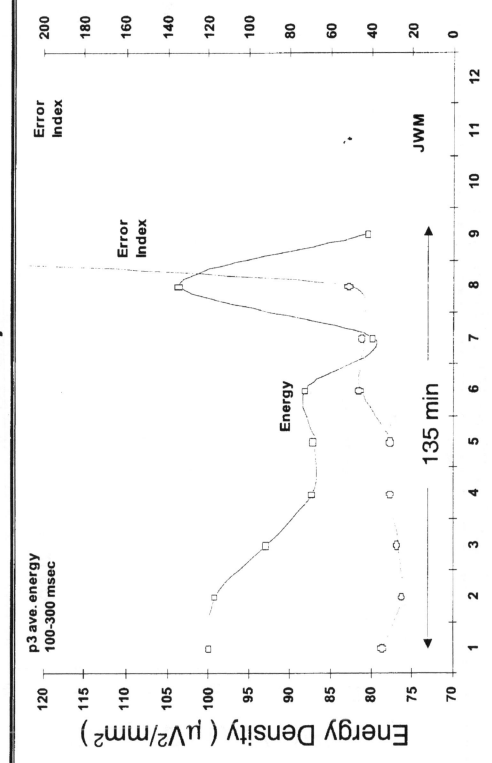

Performance & Energy Density Over Time
Subject Who Reported Feeling Sick

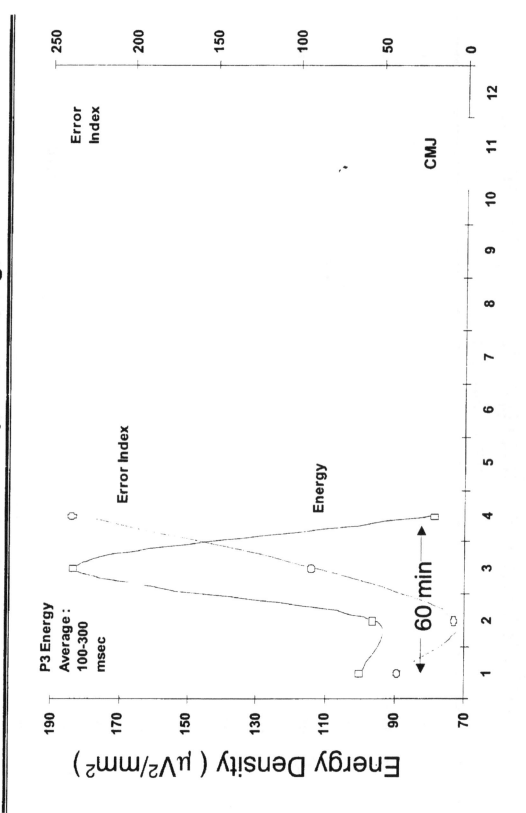

Future Plans

Improve Spatial and Computational Resolution

- 64 electrodes (128 electrodes in some subjects)
- Spline Laplacian (Nunez)
- Separate estimates of radial (gyral) and tangential (sulcal) current source densities
- Comparison of Montgomery's energy density with CSD and potential measures

Addition of irrelevant auditory probe

- Low level aperiodic random tone series
- Individual calibration
- Analysis of performance-related ERP component changes

Irrelevant Probe ERPs and Mental Effort

Electronic Warfare Simulation
(Kramer, Trejo & Humphrey, 1996)

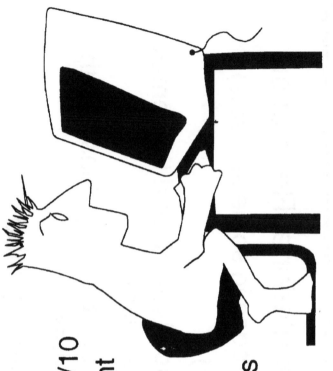

10 experienced EWs

Baseline task

- Auditory oddball 80/10/10
- Respond to one deviant tone

1-hr mission scenario

- Realistic Simulation
- Auditory oddball probes
- Variable target density over time

ERP Results with Probe Stimuli

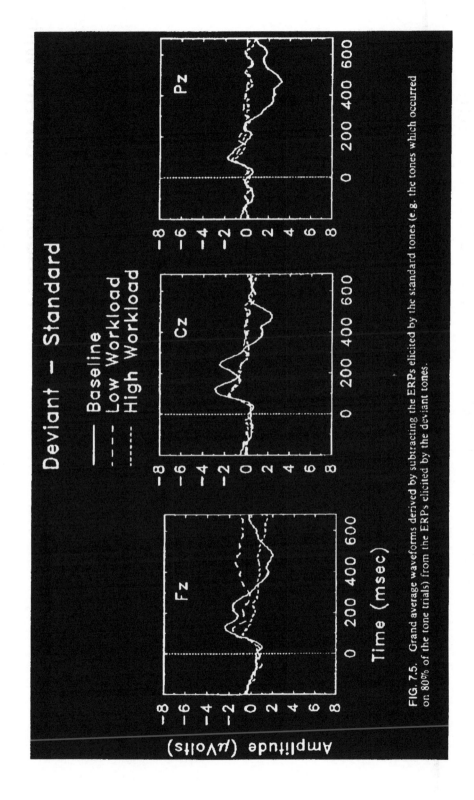

FIG. 7.5. Grand average waveforms derived by subtracting the ERPs elicited by the standard tones (e.g. the tones which occurred on 80% of the tone trials) from the ERPs elicited by the deviant tones.

Summary of Results with Probe Stimuli

Baseline task

Deviant tones
- Large N1, N2
- P3 elicited only by target deviants

Deviant vs. standard
- Mismatch negativity for both deviants

EW Simulation

Standard tones
- Reduced N1, N2

Deviant tones
- No P300
- Reduced N1, N2
- Reduced MMN

Both tone types
- Reductions covary with scenario complexity

Conclusions and Recommendations

Energy Density

- Initial data show potential onset of cognitive fatigue

- Confirm results with high-resolution source imaging and modeling, and ERP component analysis

Probe ERPs

- Prior data show tracking of mental workload

- Extend application to monitoring of cognitice fatigue

- Combine probes with mental math task and source imaging

Using EEG to Detect and Monitor Mental Fatigue

L. D. Montgomery, R. W. Montgomery, Lockheed-Martin; B. Luna, L. J. Trejo, NASA Ames Research Center, Moffett Field, CA 94035

Motivation

Theory

An event related potential (ERP) is the averaged scalp voltage potential at a particular scalp location that is generated in response to a series of like stimuli (see plots above). With multichannel ERP data, we can generate a voltage map at each sample time. From the different voltage maps we calculate a charge density map. The product of voltage and charge density is potential energy density which we call energy density.

$$L(x,v) = V(x,v)\rho(x,v) = \varepsilon v(x,v)\, V^2(x,v)$$

Experimental Methods & Results

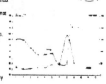

PROPOSED MODEL

$$M = 1 - H$$

$$M_N = \int (1 - H)\, dt$$

Summary

This study has concluded that the energy density analysis of the ongoing EEG may be used to investigate the mental resource allocation during mental arithmetic task performance. A quantitative EEG measure was developed which may provide insight into the allocation of mental and homeostatic effort expended in the performance of the task. A resource allocation model was developed that can be used to explain the cognitive processing that may take place during long term task performance.

This work was supported, in part, by NASA Ames Research Center Director's Discretionary Fund and the Psychological and Physiological Stressors and Factors (PPSF) Project as part of NASA's Aerospace Operations Systems Program.

For additional information please contact Leslie D. Montgomery at lmontgomery@mail.arc.nasa.gov

Suggested Reading

R. W. Montgomery, L. D. Montgomery, and R. Guisado "Cortical localization of cognitive function by regression of performance on event related potentials," Aviat. Space Environ. Med. 63, 370-374 (1992).

R. W. Montgomery, L. D. Montgomery, and R. Guisado "Electroencephalographic scalp energy analysis as a tool for investigation of cognitive performance," Journal of Biomedical Instrumentation and Technology 27(2) 137-142 (1993).

L. D. Montgomery, R. W. Montgomery, and R. Guisado "Rheoencephalographic and electroencephalographic measures of cognitive workload: Analytical procedures," Biological Psychology 40 (1-2) 143-159 (1995).

Lightning Source UK Ltd.
Milton Keynes UK
UKHW031906191218
334261UK00005B/291/P